HUMAN
BODY

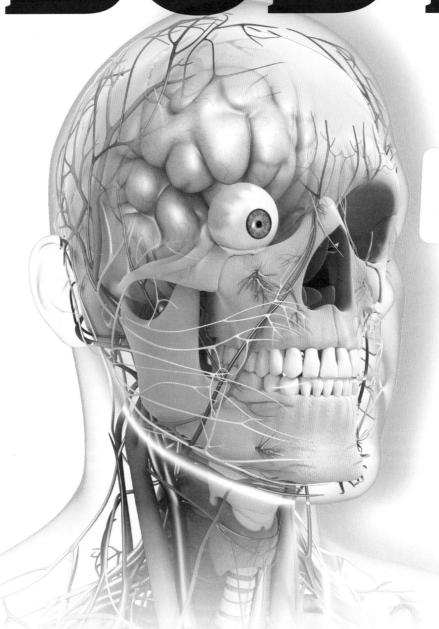

Author:
Kirsty Neale

igloobooks

CONTENTS

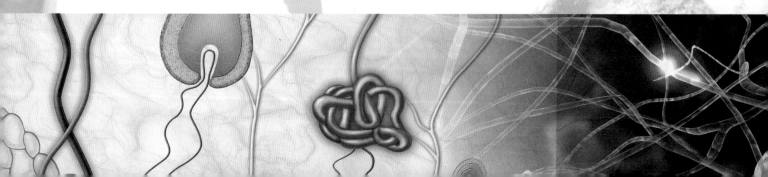

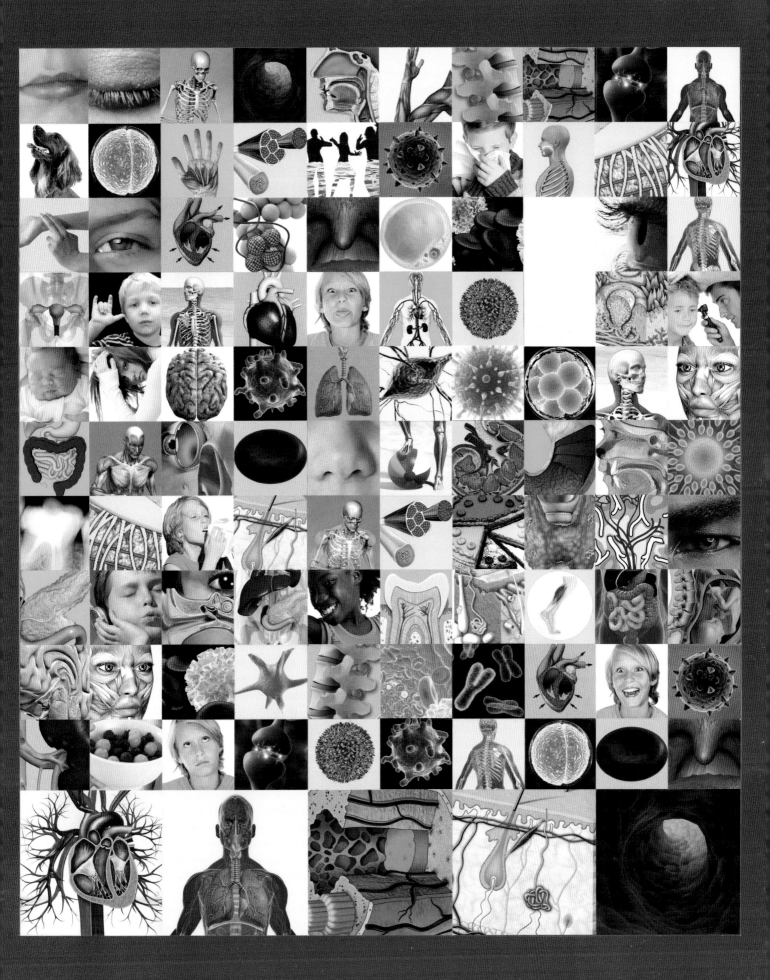

THE SKELETON

The human body is held together by a strong framework of bones, called the skeleton.

The skeleton supports our muscles and protects our organs. More than a dozen bones protect our brain and 12 pairs of ribs form a cage around our heart and lungs. As well as protecting our organs, the skeleton plays an important part in allowing us to move. The bones form levers, which muscles pull to move different parts of the body.

DID YOU KNOW?

A baby's skeleton has more than 300 bones, but an adult has only 206. This is because some of the bones fuse together as the body grows.

JOINTS

A moveable joint is where two or more bones 'join' together, but do not actually touch. They allow the skeleton to move.

Hinge
(knees and elbows)

Ball and socket
(hips and shoulders)

Gliding
(wrists and ankles)

Saddle
(thumbs)

Skull

Forehead

Upper jaw

Lower jaw

The lower jaw bone holds the lower teeth in place. It's the biggest, strongest bone in the face and the only large bone in the skull that can move.

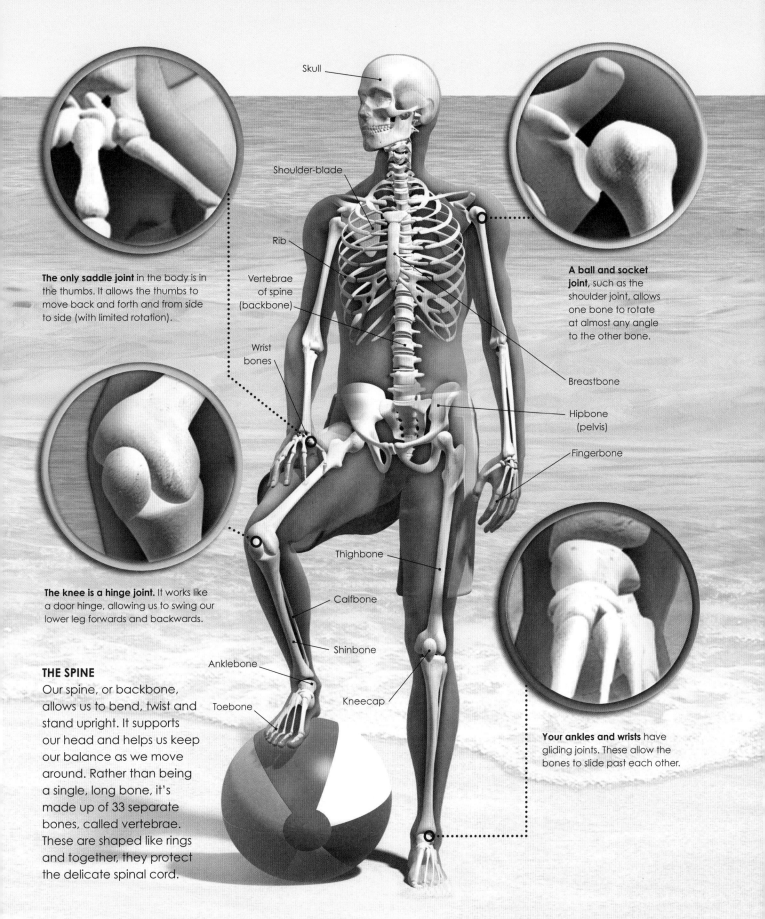

Skull

Shoulder-blade

Rib

Vertebrae
of spine
(backbone)

Wrist
bones

The only saddle joint in the body is in the thumbs. It allows the thumbs to move back and forth and from side to side (with limited rotation).

A ball and socket joint, such as the shoulder joint, allows one bone to rotate at almost any angle to the other bone.

Breastbone

Hipbone
(pelvis)

Fingerbone

The knee is a hinge joint. It works like a door hinge, allowing us to swing our lower leg forwards and backwards.

Thighbone

Calfbone

Shinbone

Anklebone

Toebone

Kneecap

Your ankles and wrists have gliding joints. These allow the bones to slide past each other.

THE SPINE

Our spine, or backbone, allows us to bend, twist and stand upright. It supports our head and helps us keep our balance as we move around. Rather than being a single, long bone, it's made up of 33 separate bones, called vertebrae. These are shaped like rings and together, they protect the delicate spinal cord.

BONES AND CELLS

The bones that make up the skeleton are strong, lightweight and full of living cells.

Cells are sometimes called the building blocks of life. They are the smallest living things on Earth and, when joined together, make up all larger living things – plants, animals and humans. Each part of your body is made from millions of cells. They come in different shapes and sizes and all have their own special job to do.

When you see a real skeleton, or bones in a museum, they look dry, crumbly and dead. But the living bones inside your body are very different. They're busy growing and changing, just like the rest of you.

CLEVER CARTILAGE

When you're born, some of your bones are made of a firm, but flexible material called cartilage. As you get older and grow, most of the cartilage becomes hard and turns into bone. Some of it stays soft though, and can be found in joints, where it stops two bones from rubbing together. You can also feel small amounts of soft cartilage at the top of your ears and at the tip of your nose.

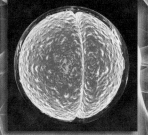

Cell divides into two

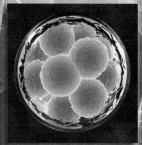

Cluster of cells

Some of the cells in the body don't live for very long. When they die, the rest of the cells need to replace them. To do this, they divide or split themselves in half, so one old cell becomes two new cells. The two new cells then divide to become a cluster of cells.

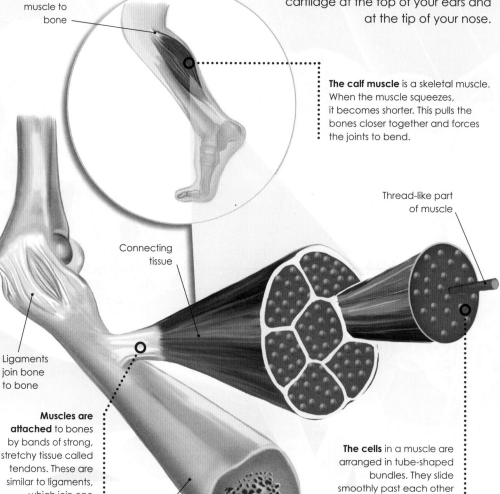

Tendons join muscle to bone

The calf muscle is a skeletal muscle. When the muscle squeezes, it becomes shorter. This pulls the bones closer together and forces the joints to bend.

Thread-like part of muscle

Connecting tissue

Ligaments join bone to bone

Muscles are attached to bones by bands of strong, stretchy tissue called tendons. These are similar to ligaments, which join one bone to another, and fascia, which connect different muscles together.

Bone

The cells in a muscle are arranged in tube-shaped bundles. They slide smoothly past each other when we squeeze and relax our muscles.

FAT CELL

When we eat, our body turns the food into energy. If we don't use all the food-energy straight away, it is stored in special fat cells called lipocytes.

BONE MARROW

Inside the hard, outer layer of many bones is a hollow space that helps to keep the skeleton light. It contains a soft, jelly-like material called bone marrow. A small amount of the bone marrow is yellow, and contains fat cells, but most of it is red. The red bone marrow makes blood cells, which carry oxygen all around the body and also help us to fight germs and disease.

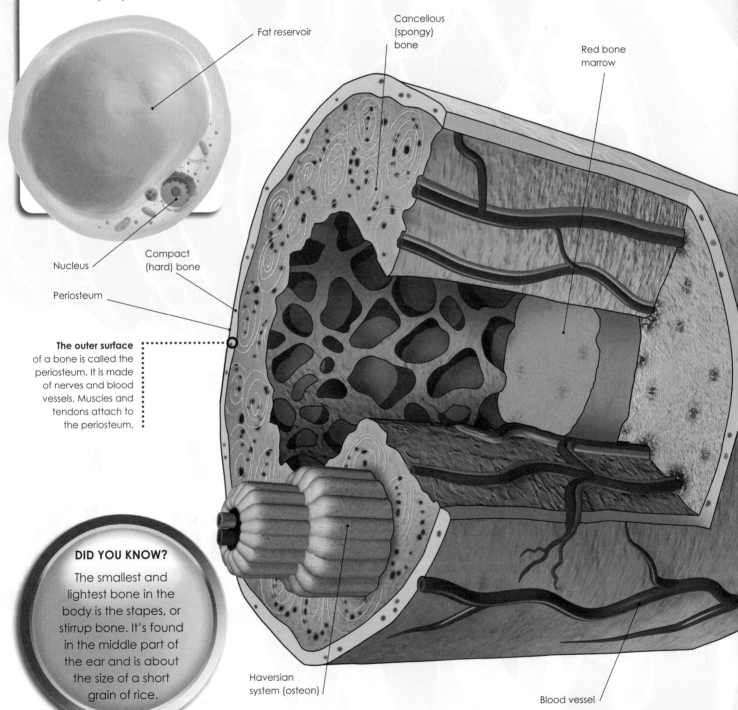

Fat reservoir

Cancellous (spongy) bone

Red bone marrow

Nucleus

Compact (hard) bone

Periosteum

The outer surface of a bone is called the periosteum. It is made of nerves and blood vessels. Muscles and tendons attach to the periosteum.

DID YOU KNOW?

The smallest and lightest bone in the body is the stapes, or stirrup bone. It's found in the middle part of the ear and is about the size of a short grain of rice.

Haversian system (osteon)

Blood vessel

MUSCLES AND MOVING

Life would be a lot less fun without muscles!

Every time we move, it's our muscles that are doing the work. We couldn't walk, talk, play games, or eat anything without them. They also take care of other important actions, such as blinking and breathing.

PULLING PAIRS

There are over 630 muscles in the body and they make up nearly half our body weight. Many of them work in groups. This is partly because muscles can only pull, they can't push. By working in pairs, two muscles can pull in opposite directions and that allows us to move parts of our body in different directions, too.

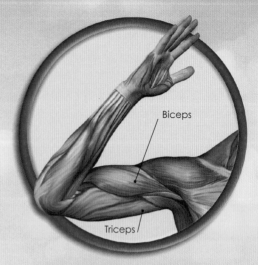

The muscles that help our arms and legs to bend are called flexors. The muscles that straighten them out again are called extensors. Biceps are flexors and triceps are extensors.

FACE MUSCLES

There are over 30 muscles in the face

Some of the muscles in the face are attached to skin, instead of bone. They help us to smile, frown, wink, raise our eyebrows, or show how we're feeling. Eye muscles are the body's busiest muscles, moving about 100,000 times each day!

Muscles let us express emotions

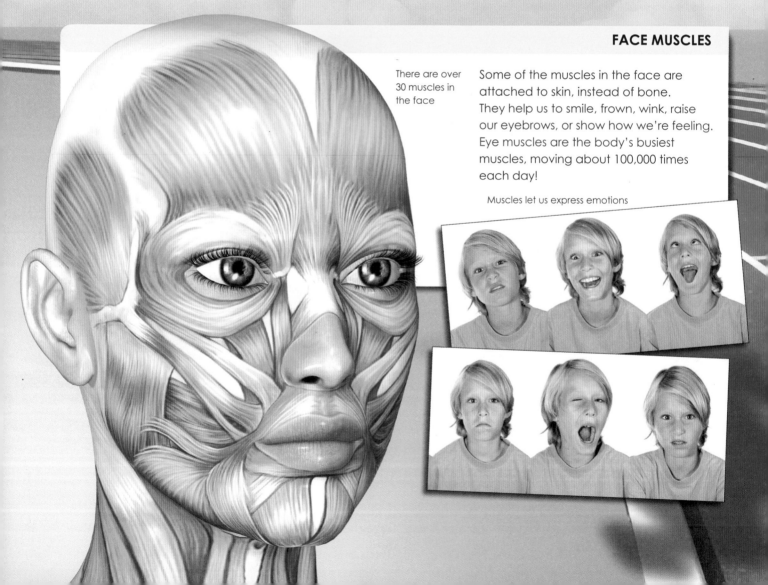

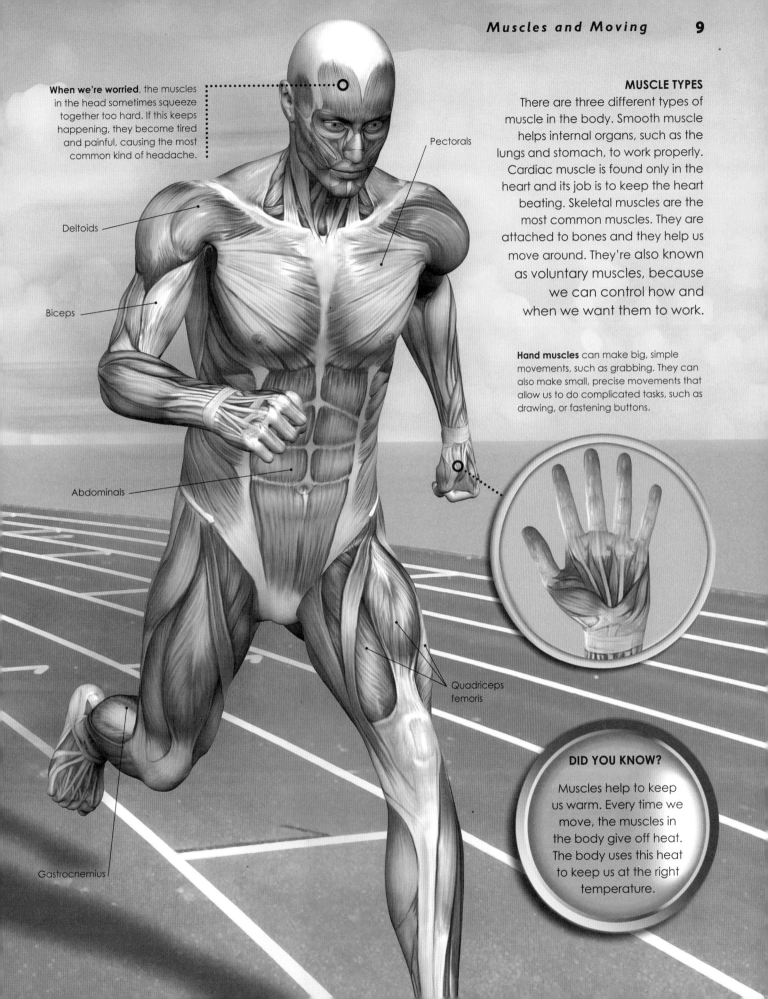

When we're worried, the muscles in the head sometimes squeeze together too hard. If this keeps happening, they become tired and painful, causing the most common kind of headache.

Deltoids

Biceps

Abdominals

Gastrocnemius

Pectorals

MUSCLE TYPES

There are three different types of muscle in the body. Smooth muscle helps internal organs, such as the lungs and stomach, to work properly. Cardiac muscle is found only in the heart and its job is to keep the heart beating. Skeletal muscles are the most common muscles. They are attached to bones and they help us move around. They're also known as voluntary muscles, because we can control how and when we want them to work.

Hand muscles can make big, simple movements, such as grabbing. They can also make small, precise movements that allow us to do complicated tasks, such as drawing, or fastening buttons.

Quadriceps femoris

DID YOU KNOW?

Muscles help to keep us warm. Every time we move, the muscles in the body give off heat. The body uses this heat to keep us at the right temperature.

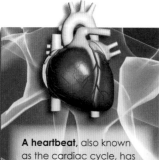

THE HEART

The heart is one of the most important organs in the body.

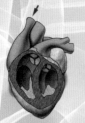

A heartbeat, also known as the cardiac cycle, has four stages.

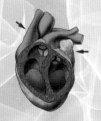

1 First, the heart relaxes and blood enters through the veins.

2 Then the atria contract, or squeeze, and force blood into the ventricles.

3 Next the ventricles contract and the blood is squeezed hard.

4 Finally, the blood is forced out through valves into the main arteries.

About the same size as a fist, it's actually a muscle. It sits in the middle of the chest, protected by the ribcage and beats all the time, even when we're asleep.

PUMPING BLOOD

The heart's main job is to pump blood around the body, delivering the oxygen it needs to keep working. The blood comes in through veins on the right side of the heart and is pumped out into the lungs. There, it's mixed with oxygen, which comes from the air we breathe. From the lungs, the blood goes into the left side of the heart, where it's pumped back out into the body.

YOUR BEATING HEART

When you feel your heart beating, it's actually the squeezing and relaxing of the heart muscle that you can feel. Inside the heart, four valves open and close to allow the movement of blood. The regular 'thud' of your heartbeat is made by the valves as they close.

The heart is divided into four separate areas, or chambers. The two at the top are called atria (the left atrium and right atrium) and the two below are ventricles.

DID YOU KNOW?

People used to think that feelings came from the heart, but it's really the brain that controls how fast the heart beats when a person is feeling happy, sad, or scared.

TAKING A PULSE

Doctors 'take' or measure a pulse to find out if a patient's heart is beating too fast, or too slow. One way to do this is to press two fingers against the artery in the wrist and count the number of heartbeats, or pulses, you can feel the heart make in one minute. Each beat is a blood pressure bulge from the heart that is carried along the artery.

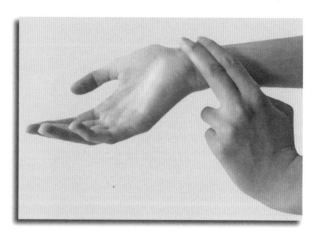

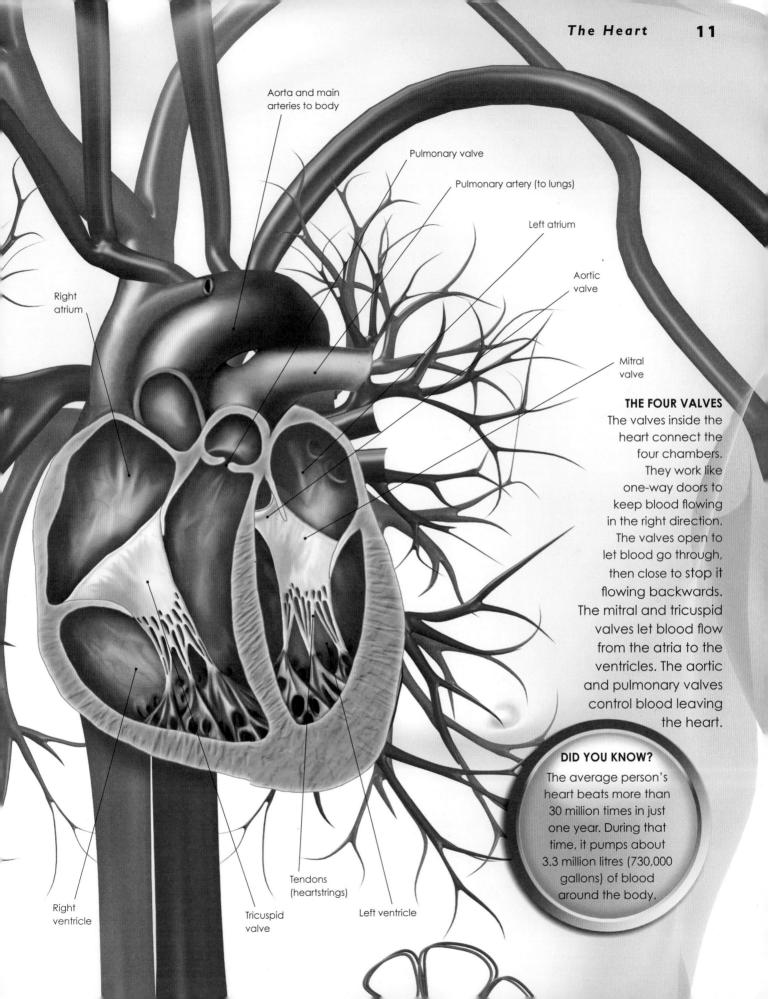

Aorta and main
arteries to body

Pulmonary valve

Pulmonary artery (to lungs)

Left atrium

Aortic
valve

Right
atrium

Mitral
valve

THE FOUR VALVES
The valves inside the
heart connect the
four chambers.
They work like
one-way doors to
keep blood flowing
in the right direction.
The valves open to
let blood go through,
then close to stop it
flowing backwards.
The mitral and tricuspid
valves let blood flow
from the atria to the
ventricles. The aortic
and pulmonary valves
control blood leaving
the heart.

DID YOU KNOW?
The average person's
heart beats more than
30 million times in just
one year. During that
time, it pumps about
3.3 million litres (730,000
gallons) of blood
around the body.

Tendons
(heartstrings)

Right
ventricle

Tricuspid
valve

Left ventricle

Blood is made up of red cells, white cells and platelets floating in a watery, yellow liquid, called plasma. A single drop of blood contains over 5 million cells.

Red blood cells carry oxygen. They live for about 120 days.

White blood cells help defend the body against illness. They attack and destroy any germs that enter the body.

Platelets are cells that repair broken blood vessels. They stick together, or clot, when you cut yourself to stop the bleeding.

Blood, veins and arteries

Together, veins and arteries are known as blood vessels.

Blood travels through tube-shaped blood vessels to reach cells all over the body. It delivers oxygen and takes away waste, keeping the cells and body healthy.

RED AND BLUE

The blood in our veins is a darker shade of red than the blood in our arteries. This is because it contains less oxygen. So, why do the veins under the surface of the skin look blue? Veins are actually white, but the effect of dark red blood flowing through them and skin on top, makes them appear blue.

Heart

Blood vessel

The cardiovascular system is made up of our heart, blood and blood vessels. It works so efficiently that each blood cell takes just twenty seconds to circle the whole body.

Arteries are like hoses with thick, stretchy walls. They carry blood away from the heart. Veins are usually thinner. They take blood and waste back towards the heart.

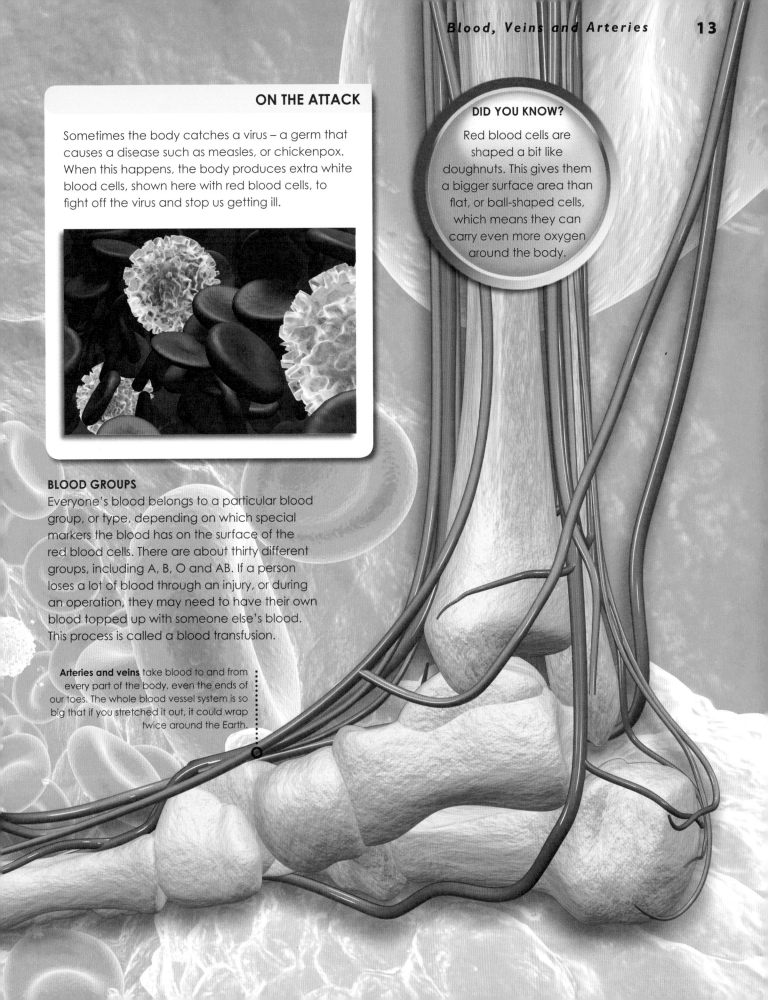

ON THE ATTACK

Sometimes the body catches a virus – a germ that causes a disease such as measles, or chickenpox. When this happens, the body produces extra white blood cells, shown here with red blood cells, to fight off the virus and stop us getting ill.

DID YOU KNOW?

Red blood cells are shaped a bit like doughnuts. This gives them a bigger surface area than flat, or ball-shaped cells, which means they can carry even more oxygen around the body.

BLOOD GROUPS

Everyone's blood belongs to a particular blood group, or type, depending on which special markers the blood has on the surface of the red blood cells. There are about thirty different groups, including A, B, O and AB. If a person loses a lot of blood through an injury, or during an operation, they may need to have their own blood topped up with someone else's blood. This process is called a blood transfusion.

Arteries and veins take blood to and from every part of the body, even the ends of our toes. The whole blood vessel system is so big that if you stretched it out, it could wrap twice around the Earth.

TAKING A BREATH

Lungs allow our body to take in fresh air and get rid of stale air.

The body is brilliant at making sure our lungs and airways are kept clear, so we can breathe easily.

When we cough, it's usually because there's something in our lungs which shouldn't be there, such as dust, smoke, or an infection. Coughing forces air out of the lungs, as the body tries to get rid of the irritation.

A sneeze happens if something irritates our nose. The lungs force air out in a sneeze, instead of a cough.

Hiccups happen when our diaphragm is over-working. Extra air rushes into the lungs and as it hits the voicebox – hic!

Fresh air contains oxygen and lungs work with the cardiovascular system to send it all around the body. Stale air is then brought back to the lungs and expelled as we breathe out.

TAKE A BREATH
Our lungs take up almost all of the space in our chest. They work together with a large muscle called the diaphragm, which sits underneath the ribcage. When we breathe in, air goes down through our windpipe into two big tubes, known as bronchi. Each bronchi branches off inside the lungs into more tubes, which gradually get smaller. The thinnest tubes are called bronchioli and each one leads into a tiny air sac, or alveolus.

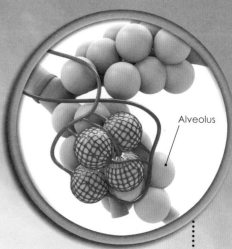

Alveolus

Inside each of our lungs we have about 300 million alveoli, or air sacs. Every time we take a breath, the alveoli fill with air, making our lungs expand like a balloon.

BREATHING IN AND OUT

When you breathe in, your diaphragm squashes itself flat and your ribs lift upwards. This gives your lungs room to inflate. When you breathe out again, your diaphragm relaxes, your ribs move down and the air is pushed back out.

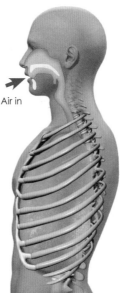

Air in

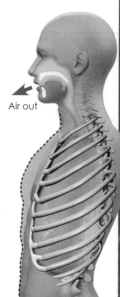

Air out

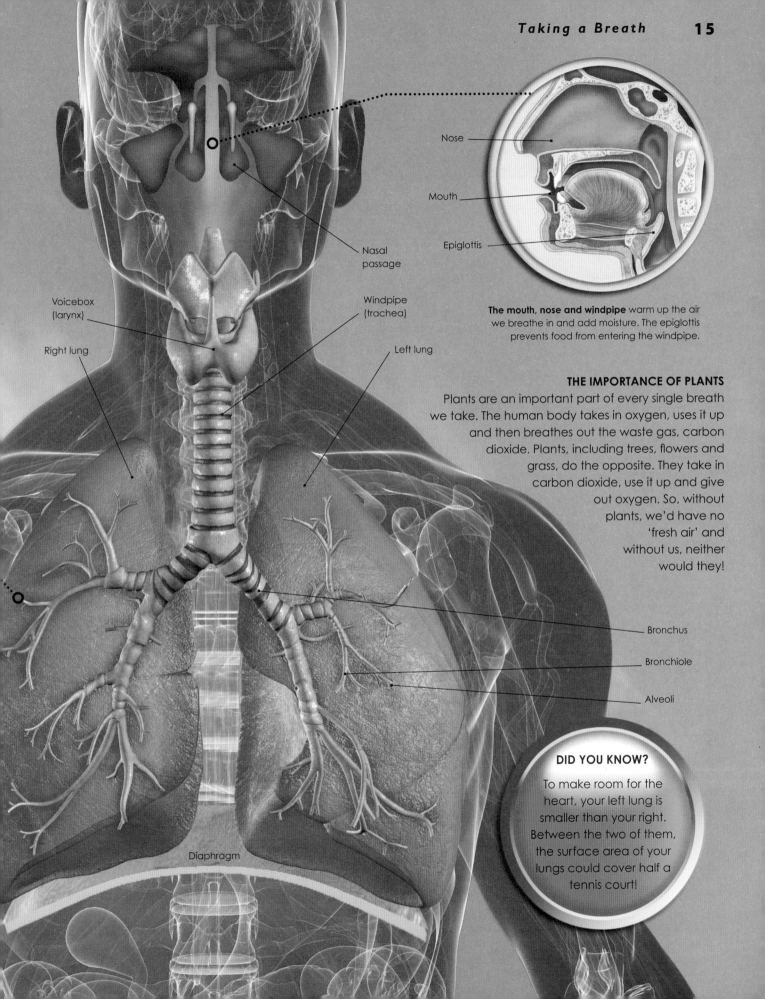

Nose

Mouth

Epiglottis

The mouth, nose and windpipe warm up the air we breathe in and add moisture. The epiglottis prevents food from entering the windpipe.

Nasal passage

Voicebox (larynx)

Windpipe (trachea)

Right lung

Left lung

Bronchus

Bronchiole

Alveoli

Diaphragm

THE IMPORTANCE OF PLANTS

Plants are an important part of every single breath we take. The human body takes in oxygen, uses it up and then breathes out the waste gas, carbon dioxide. Plants, including trees, flowers and grass, do the opposite. They take in carbon dioxide, use it up and give out oxygen. So, without plants, we'd have no 'fresh air' and without us, neither would they!

DID YOU KNOW?

To make room for the heart, your left lung is smaller than your right. Between the two of them, the surface area of your lungs could cover half a tennis court!

THE BRAIN

Inside our skull is an amazing, complicated and powerful super-computer.

Our brain is in charge of almost everything that goes on in the rest of the body. It controls muscles, organs, senses, the way we feel and is also home to all the things we know and remember.

Emotions, such as sadness, or joy, are often said to come from the heart, but they actually come from the brain. Scientists have discovered that two almond-shaped groups of cells called the amygdala are the part of the brain involved in feelings.

MIND MATTERS

It might not look very impressive, but the lumpy, walnut-shaped human brain is so complicated that scientists still don't know everything about the way it works. It has evolved over millions of years and is made up of billions of cells. To work in the most efficient way, the brain is divided into different areas. Some parts are used for storing memories, some parts help us to learn and solve problems, some parts control groups of muscles and other parts are in charge of speech.

When the brain recognizes an emotion, it sends signals telling the rest of the body how to act. Happy feelings can curve our lips into a smile, while feelings of anger might make us frown, or shout.

LEFT AND RIGHT SIDES OF THE BRAIN

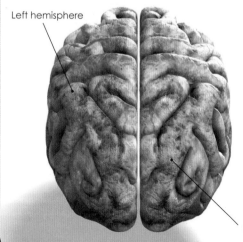

Left hemisphere

Right hemisphere

The brain is divided into two sides, or hemispheres. The left side of the brain controls the right side of the body and the right side of the brain controls the left side of the body. A big fold divides the two parts of the brain, but they are connected by a thick bundle of nerves at the base of the brain.

PARTS OF THE BRAIN

Over three-quarters of the brain is made up of the cerebrum. This is the part we use for thinking, remembering and solving problems. It also controls our voluntary muscles. The cerebellum is much smaller. It takes care of balance and coordination. Each of these brain parts is joined to the spinal cord by the brain stem. The stem looks after our involuntary muscles and controls things such as breathing and heartbeat.

THE NERVOUS SYSTEM

The nerves, brain and spinal cord make up the nervous system. They work together to send messages around the whole body.

The nerves gather information – maybe from something felt, or touched – and pass it along the spinal cord to the brain. The brain then sends messages back out so the body can act on the information.

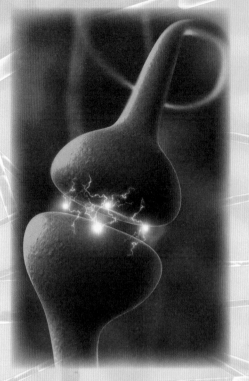

WHAT ARE NERVES?

The nervous system contains billions of tiny nerve cells called neurons. Each individual nerve is like a thread, made up of neurons bundled together. The biggest nerves are over 2 cm (0.8 in) thick and the smallest are thinner than a human hair. There are two main types of neuron in the body – sensory neurons and motor neurons. Sensory neurons send messages to the brain about the outside world, and how we're feeling. Motor neurons pass information from the brain to the muscles.

Central nervous system (brain and spinal cord)

When a neuron is excited, either by the senses, or by chemicals in the body, it gives off a small spark of electricity called a nerve impulse. These nerve impulses 'jump' from one neuron to the next across a small gap called a synapse.

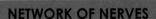

NETWORK OF NERVES

The nervous system has two main parts – the central nervous system, made up of the brain and spinal cord, and the peripheral nervous system, made up of nerves passing to all parts of the body. If someone has an injury and their nerves become damaged, they may feel pain, numbness, or even paralysis (their muscles stop working).

Peripheral nervous system (nerves)

DID YOU KNOW?

Nerves don't just act on messages from external senses (sight, sound, hearing, touch and taste). They also take care of senses inside the body, such as hunger and thirst.

Our eyes are well protected. They sit inside deep sockets under a tough brow bone. But this is only the start of the clever protection system.

Our eyelids shut quickly if anything threatens our eyes, or comes too close to the eyeballs. They also protect against very bright light.

Eyelashes grow above and below the eye. They trap specks of dust and dirt and keep them out of our eyes.

Eyebrows stop sweat and other types of moisture from running off our forehead and into our eyes.

Looking at Eyes

Eyes let the body take in all sorts of information about the outside world.

Wherever we are, whatever we're doing, our eyes are busy collecting images to send to the brain. As well as seeing every shade of the rainbow, they also see light, movement and shapes, helping us make sense of our surroundings.

PARTS OF THE EYE

The clear, glassy dome at the front of the eye is called the cornea. It sits on top of the blue, brown, or green iris. In the middle of each eye, the black pupil is actually an opening in the iris. It shrinks and expands to control how much light enters the eye.

INSIDE THE EYE

Behind the pupil is a clear lens. It focuses light onto the retina at the back of the eye. Special cells in the retina, called rods, turn the light into a shaded image. More cells, called cones, work out if the image is yellow, green, violet, or another shade. The eye then sends the picture it sees along the optic nerve to the brain.

IT'S OK TO CRY!

Every time we blink, our eye produces tears. The eyelids wash the tears over the eyeballs to stop them drying out and to rinse away any specks of dust, or dirt.

Tears

The image on the retina is upside down, but the brain translates the picture so we 'see' it the right way up.

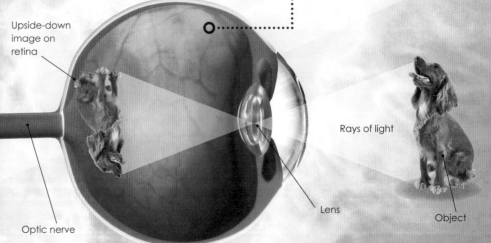

Upside-down image on retina

Optic nerve

Lens

Rays of light

Object

SPECTACULAR MUSCLES!
The lenses in our eyes use muscles to focus, or get a clear picture. As the muscles squeeze and relax, they change the shape of the lens, allowing us to see things nearby, or far away. Some people have lenses that don't focus properly. Pictures fall too far in front of, or behind the retina and look blurry. To fix this problem, people wear glasses.

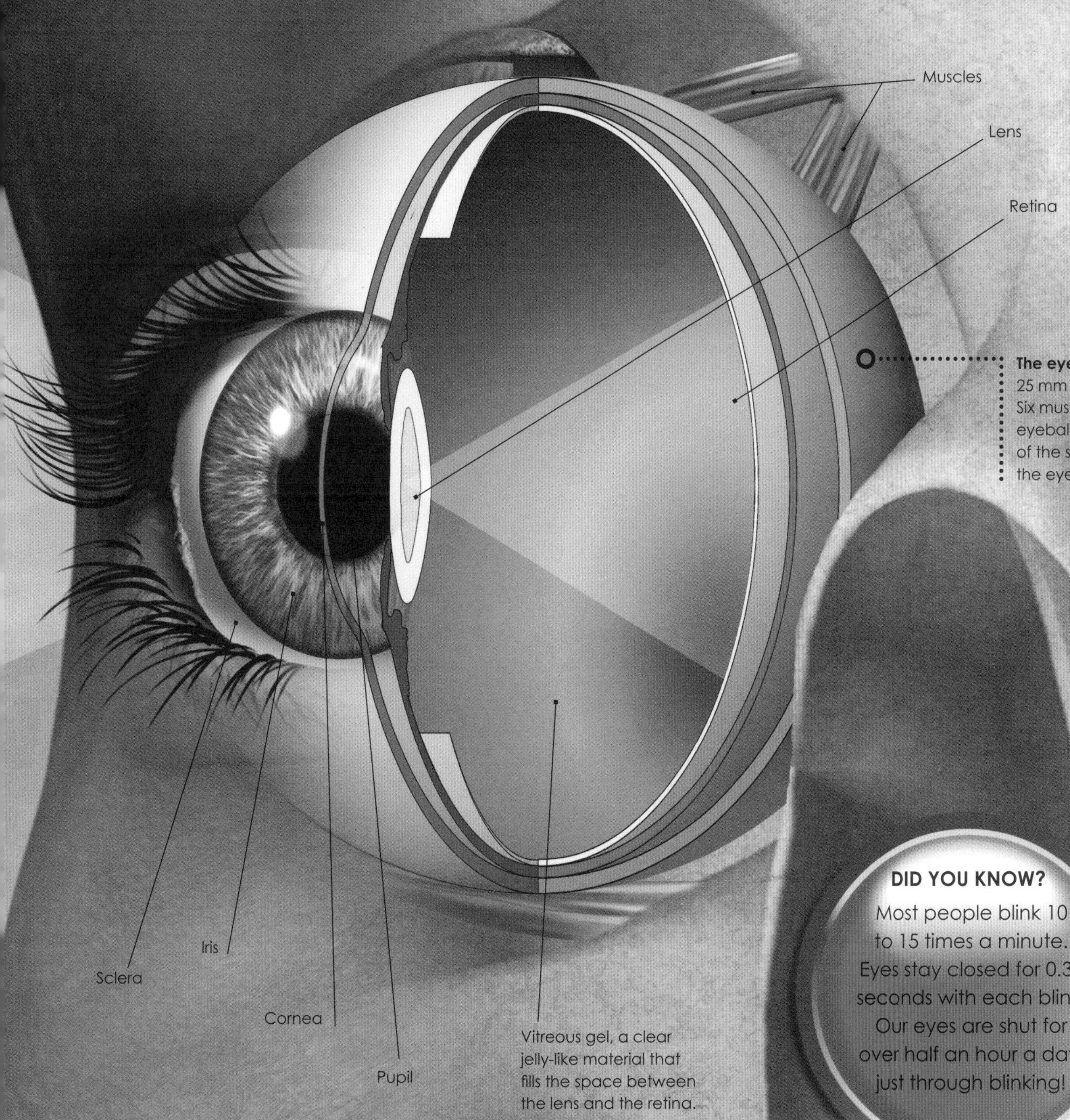

Muscles

Lens

Retina

The eyeball is about 25 mm (1 inch) across. Six muscles attach the eyeball to the bones of the socket behind the eye.

Iris

Sclera

Cornea

Pupil

Vitreous gel, a clear jelly-like material that fills the space between the lens and the retina.

DID YOU KNOW?
Most people blink 10 to 15 times a minute. Eyes stay closed for 0.35 seconds with each blink. Our eyes are shut for over half an hour a day, just through blinking!

Outer ear (auricle)

Hear, hear!

Ears aren't just for listening and hearing, they also help us keep our balance.

These clever organs collect sounds and pass them to the brain, which makes sense of them.

HOW DO WE HEAR?

When something makes a noise, it sends vibrations, known as sound waves, through the air. The vibrations reach the outer ear, which funnels them through the ear canal to the eardrum. When they reach the eardrum, it vibrates and starts a chain reaction, sending the vibrations to the middle ear and then the inner ear.

GETTING THE MESSAGE

In the inner ear is a shell-shaped part called the cochlea. The cochlea is filled with liquid and lined with cells covered in tiny hairs. As the liquid vibrates, it moves the hairs. The hairs then send nerve signals to the brain, which translates the vibrations into sound messages.

HEARING LOSS

Deafness and loss of hearing have many different causes. People can be born completely deaf, or become hard of hearing later in life. Some people who can't hear normal speech use sign language to communicate instead.

In American sign language, this symbol means 'I love you.'

Feeling dizzy and losing our balance are sensations created partly in our ears. Above the cochlea are three tubes, called semicircular canals, containing liquid and hair-covered cells. When our head moves, the liquid moves, too. The cells send signals to the brain, which adjusts our balance. If we spin round very quickly, the signals can get confused and make us feel dizzy.

Sometimes our ears pop! This happens when the air pressure inside our ears changes, for example, when we enter a tunnel at high speed. To balance this out, some of the air escapes along a special tube, called the Eustachian tube. The 'pop' happens when the tube opens and the air is released.

WONDERFUL WAX

Our body produces earwax to keep our ears clean and well-protected. It's made by glands in the ear canal. As well as stopping the skin in our ears from getting dry and itchy, it keeps out dust, dirt and even small insects!

Ears can become blocked by earwax. A doctor can check this by shining a bright light into our ears to see inside.

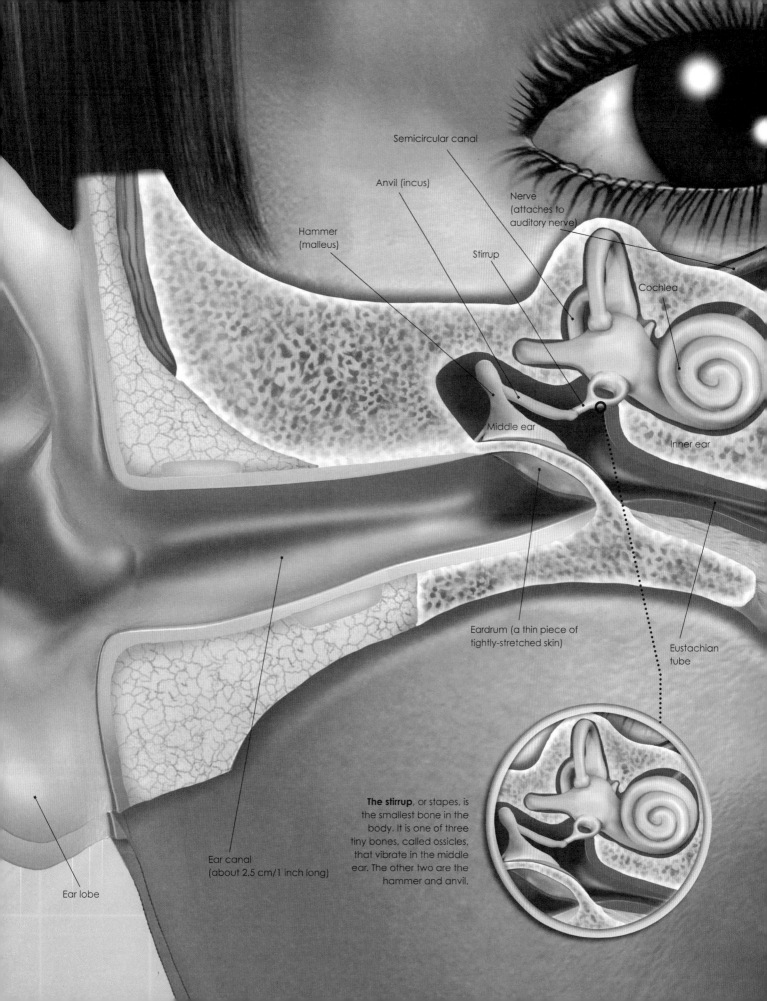

Semicircular canal

Anvil (incus)

Nerve
(attaches to
auditory nerve)

Hammer
(malleus)

Stirrup

Cochlea

Middle ear

Inner ear

Eardrum (a thin piece of
tightly-stretched skin)

Eustachian
tube

The stirrup, or stapes, is
the smallest bone in the
body. It is one of three
tiny bones, called ossicles,
that vibrate in the middle
ear. The other two are the
hammer and anvil.

Ear canal
(about 2.5 cm/1 inch long)

Ear lobe

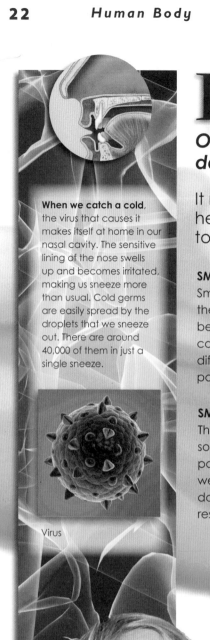

When we catch a cold, the virus that causes it makes itself at home in our nasal cavity. The sensitive lining of the nose swells up and becomes irritated, making us sneeze more than usual. Cold germs are easily spread by the droplets that we sneeze out. There are around 40,000 of them in just a single sneeze.

Virus

HOW DO WE SMELL?

Our nose can sniff out all kinds of things, from danger to tasty snacks.

It might seem less important than seeing and hearing, but our sense of smell is every bit as vital to the way we live and enjoy our life.

SMELL THAT!

Smells are made up of tiny scent particles in the air. When we sniff, they flow into the cavity behind the nose. The upper lining of the nasal cavity contains millions of cells that recognize different scent particles. When they sense a particular smell, a signal is sent to the brain.

SMELL AND THE BRAIN

The olfactory cortex is the part of the brain that sorts out smells. It communicates with other parts of the brain to work out exactly what we can smell. If it's something that could be dangerous, such as fire, our brain prepares the rest of our body to act, too.

DID YOU KNOW?

Our sense of smell helps us taste food better. Try putting it to the test – block out smells by pinching your nose, then eat a mouthful of food and see how it tastes.

Our sense of smell is closely linked to memory. The brain uses this link and always connects new smells to a particular memory.

Sometimes people sneeze when they look at a bright light. Doctors think this happens because of a mix-up in the signals sent between the eyes, nose and brain.

SNEEZING

When we sneeze, it's usually because something has tickled or irritated the inside of our nose. Our body goes through an incredible process, just to get rid of what might be a few tiny particles of dust. The tickle in the nose sends a message to the brain, which then sends its own message to muscles in the stomach, chest, throat and face. The muscles work together in exactly the right order to form a sneeze and blast the ticklish particles out of the nose. It's difficult to measure, but experts think that a sneeze travels at between 80 and 160 km per hour (50 and 100 miles per hour) as it leaves the nose.

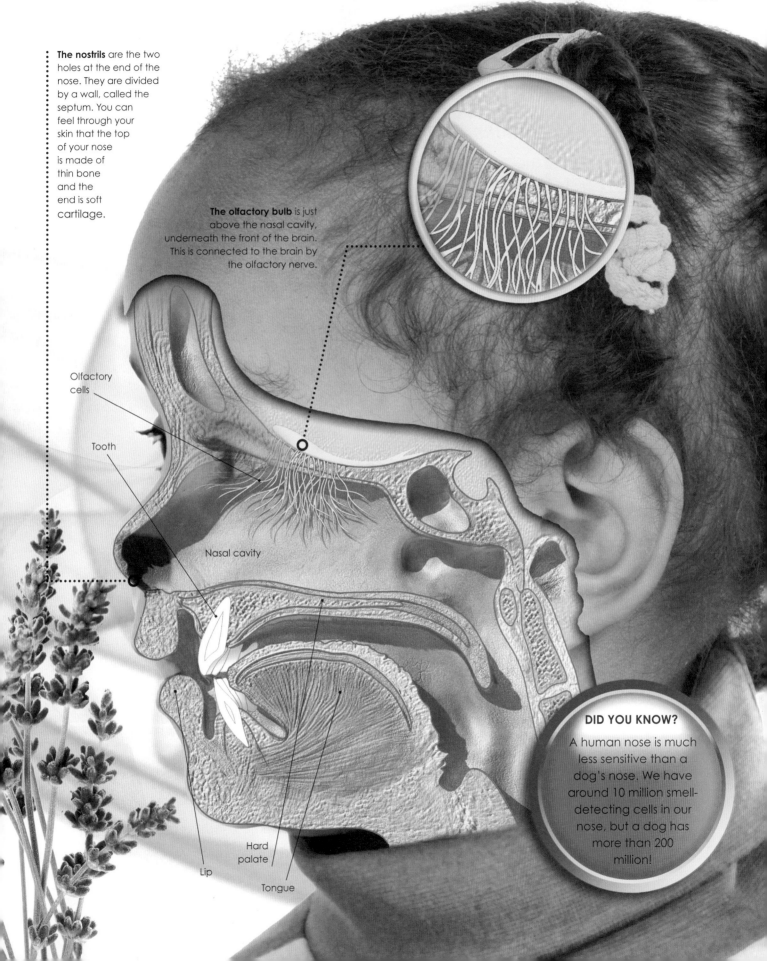

The nostrils are the two holes at the end of the nose. They are divided by a wall, called the septum. You can feel through your skin that the top of your nose is made of thin bone and the end is soft cartilage.

The olfactory bulb is just above the nasal cavity, underneath the front of the brain. This is connected to the brain by the olfactory nerve.

Olfactory cells

Tooth

Nasal cavity

Lip

Hard palate

Tongue

DID YOU KNOW?

A human nose is much less sensitive than a dog's nose. We have around 10 million smell-detecting cells in our nose, but a dog has more than 200 million!

MEGA MOUTHS

We can do all sorts of wonderful things with our mouth – taste, talk, sing, whistle and even kiss!

The mouth works together with the teeth and tongue so we can chew and swallow food. Teamed with our lungs, it also lets us make sounds, from the quietest whisper to screams and shouts.

Lips are covered with a very thin layer of skin – thinner than on the rest of the face. This means that the blood vessels underneath show through more easily, so our lips look dark pink or, in cold weather, when blood flow is slower, purple-ish blue.

We often have to purse our lips to make certain words and sounds. We also have to purse our lips to whistle.

SPIT IT OUT!
Saliva, or spit, plays an important part in keeping the mouth healthy. Without it, the tongue would very quickly dry out and our tastebuds would stop working. The chemicals in saliva help to keep the mouth naturally clean and free from germs. It also works with the tongue and teeth to break down food, ready for us to swallow.

SAY HELLO
Our voicebox, or larynx, is in the throat. As we breathe, air goes through the larynx and over two small folds, called vocal chords. Muscles in the larynx squeeze the vocal chords together when we speak and the air causes them to vibrate. The mouth makes the noise louder, like a speaker, and the teeth and tongue shape the sounds into words.

DID YOU KNOW?
The tongue is mostly made up of strong skeletal muscles, and is home to about 10,000 tastebuds. Just like fingerprints, everyone's tongue-print is unique!

The muscles in and around the lips help us eat, whistle, smile, sip drinks through a straw and form letters such as 'p' and 'w' when we talk.

TASTEBUDS

Tastebuds are clumps of cells all over the surface of the tongue that act like tiny sensors. They send messages to the brain, which then works out what we are tasting. The five basic types of taste are sweet, salty, sour, bitter and savory (umami).

Sweet

Salty

Savory (umami)

Sour

Bitter

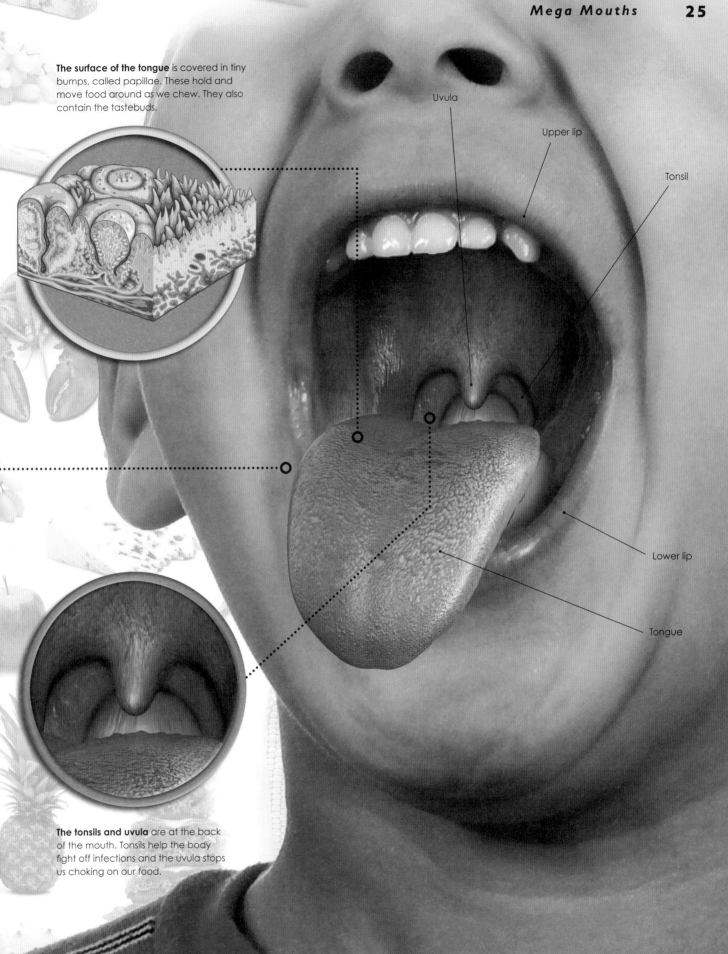

The surface of the tongue is covered in tiny bumps, called papillae. These hold and move food around as we chew. They also contain the tastebuds.

Uvula

Upper lip

Tonsil

Lower lip

Tongue

The tonsils and uvula are at the back of the mouth. Tonsils help the body fight off infections and the uvula stops us choking on our food.

AMAZING SKIN

Strong and stretchy, the skin is the body's protective cover and largest organ.

As well as holding bones, muscles and organs inside, our skin also keeps out germs. It allows us to touch and feel and even repairs itself when damaged.

NEW SKIN
Skin has two main layers. In the lower layer, or dermis, there are nerve-endings, blood vessels and glands. The upper layer, or epidermis, is where new skin cells are made. Once the cells are ready, they rise to the top of the epidermis and take the place of older, dead cells. The dead cells fall off. We shed millions of them every day, but there are always new cells waiting to replace them.

Body temperature is controlled by blood vessels, hair, sweat glands and skin. If you're too hot, blood vessels widen to increase the blood flow and you begin to sweat. This releases heat from inside the body and as sweat evaporates, it also cools the skin.

Hot and sweaty

When you're cold, blood vessels shrink to keep warm blood away from the chilly surface of your skin. Tiny hairs on the skin stand up to trap heat. This also puckers the skin, causing goosebumps.

Feeling cold

Some of the cells in our skin make a chemical called melanin. This is what makes the skin dark or light. Dark-skinned people have more melanin than those with fair skin.

Hair shaft

Epidermis

Sweat pore

Dermis

Sweat gland

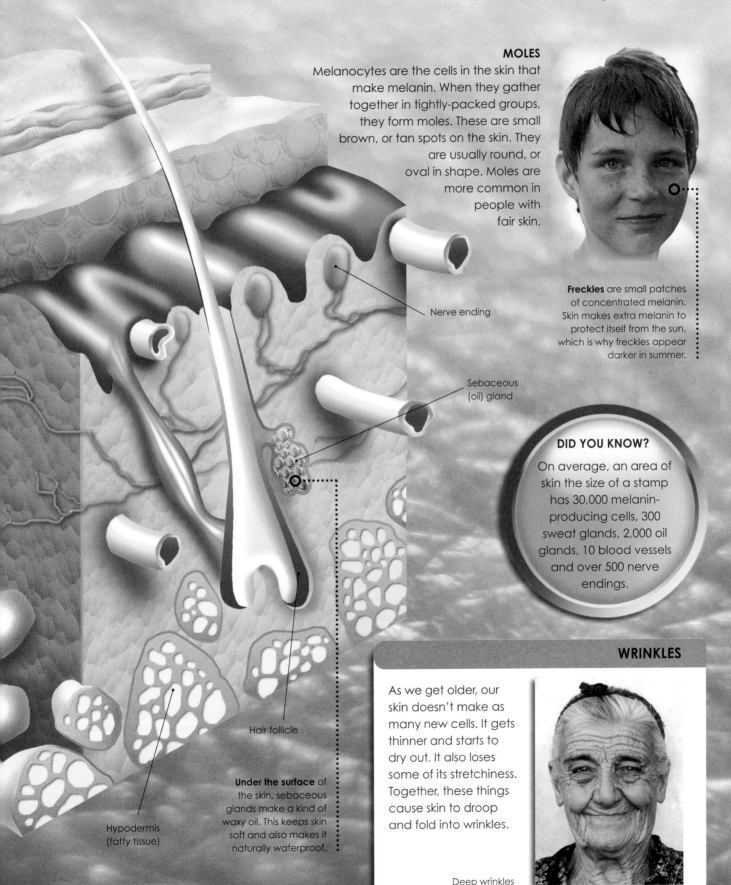

MOLES

Melanocytes are the cells in the skin that make melanin. When they gather together in tightly-packed groups, they form moles. These are small brown, or tan spots on the skin. They are usually round, or oval in shape. Moles are more common in people with fair skin.

Freckles are small patches of concentrated melanin. Skin makes extra melanin to protect itself from the sun, which is why freckles appear darker in summer.

Nerve ending

Sebaceous (oil) gland

DID YOU KNOW?

On average, an area of skin the size of a stamp has 30,000 melanin-producing cells, 300 sweat glands, 2,000 oil glands, 10 blood vessels and over 500 nerve endings.

Hair follicle

Under the surface of the skin, sebaceous glands make a kind of waxy oil. This keeps skin soft and also makes it naturally waterproof.

Hypodermis (fatty tissue)

WRINKLES

As we get older, our skin doesn't make as many new cells. It gets thinner and starts to dry out. It also loses some of its stretchiness. Together, these things cause skin to droop and fold into wrinkles.

Deep wrinkles

HOW WE BEGIN

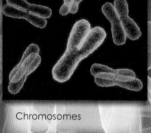
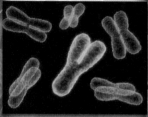

Long strands of genes are known as chromosomes. Each of our cells has 46 chromosomes – 23 from our mother and 23 from our father.

Chromosomes

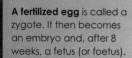

Egg and sperm

When a male sperm, or seed, and a female egg join together, the egg is fertilized. It becomes the first cell of a brand new person.

Everybody, no matter who they are, or where they come from, starts life in the same way.

Beginning with a single cell, it takes about 40 weeks for a baby to grow inside its mother. It lives and develops inside the womb, which protects the baby until it's ready to be born.

THE WOMB
The womb, or uterus, is an amazing organ. It sits in the abdomen and is normally about the size of a chicken's egg. However, as a baby begins to grow, so does the womb. It gradually stretches to makes a safe, comfortable home for the baby, right up until it's ready to be born. By then, an average baby weighs about 3.2 kg (7 lbs) and measures 35–50 cm (13–20 inches) long – much bigger than a chicken's egg! Sometimes, babies are born too early. It's a lot harder for them to survive and carry on growing in the outside world than it is inside the womb.

A fertilized egg is called a zygote. It then becomes an embryo and, after 8 weeks, a fetus (or foetus).

5 days   21 days   28 days   48 days   56 days   12 weeks   16 weeks   6 months   8 months

GROWING CELLS

Once an egg has been fertilized, it moves along the fallopian tube and into the womb. There, it starts to divide. First, it splits in half, so one cell becomes two. Those two cells split in half, to make four, and these then divide and make eight. The cells keep splitting until there are billions of them. They then begin to move around and arrange themselves in the right place, as they grow into a baby.

Inside the womb, a baby is joined to its mother by the umbilical cord. This provides oxygen and nutrients to help it grow.

Genes in our cells, contain the information needed to build a new person and new cells. They're made from a material called DNA.

SCAN

Doctors can look at a baby inside the womb using sound-waves and echoes. A computer turns the sound into pictures, so the doctor can see the baby and make sure it's growing properly.

Scan of a baby inside the womb

Amniotic fluid

Placenta

Umbilical cord

Muscle (rectus abdominis)

Womb (uterus)

Fetus

Cervix

Birth canal

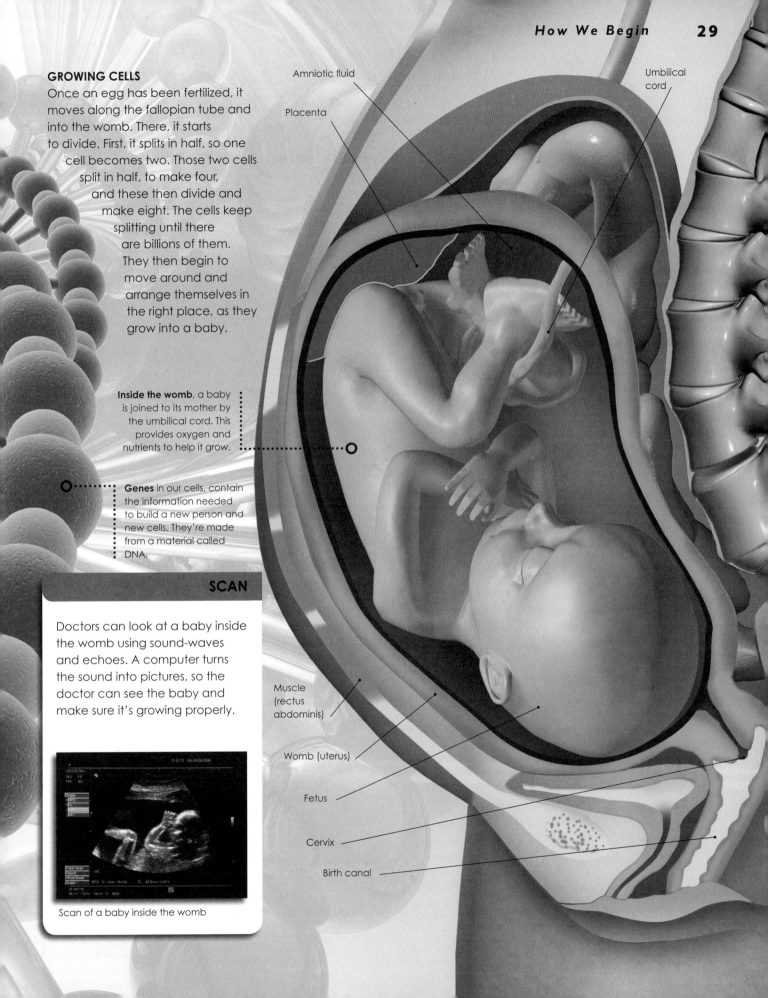

GLOSSARY

Abdomen Part of the body between the chest and hipbone containing the stomach and major organs.

Bloodstream The flow of blood around the body.

Cardiovascular Relating to the heart and blood vessels (also known as the circulatory system).

Cartilage Strong, but flexible material found in areas of the body including the ears, nose, knees and joints.

Cavity A hole, or hollow space.

Cell The smallest unit of life – all living things are made up of cells.

Cuticle A thin, u-shaped piece of skin at the base of finger and toenails.

Dentin Tough, bone-like material that makes up part of a tooth.

DNA A chemical in every cell that controls the cell's shape, purpose and the way it behaves.

Epiglottis A flap of tissue at the bottom of the tongue that stops food going into the windpipe.

Evaporate, evaporation A process in which a liquid, such as water, is turned into a gas by heating it.

External On the outside of the body.

Fallopian tubes Two tubes that connect the ovaries to the womb in females.

Germ A tiny, single-cell life-form that often spreads disease.

Gland An organ that makes a particular chemical, or substance to be released inside, or outside the body. Hormones and sweat are made by glands.

Haversian system (osteon) Tiny, tube-shaped bundles of tissue that make up compact bone.

Immune Protected against, or not at risk from, a particular type of germ, or a disease, such as measles.

Infection A disease caused by a germ that gets inside the body and begins to multiply.

Internal On the inside of the body.

Involuntary An action that takes place without us choosing, or deciding to do it.

Keratin A tough chemical substance and the main element in our hair and nails.

Long-sighted A problem with the eyes that stops a person seeing an object clearly if the object is too close to them.

Melanin A pigment found in hair, skin and eyes. One type of melanin causes red hair and freckles.

Nucleus The part of a cell that controls the rest of the cell.

Nutrients Chemicals, often obtained from food, that a plant, or animal needs in order to live and grow.

Olfactory Relating to smells, or the sense of smell.

Organ A part of the body that has a particular job to do. Ears are external organs and the heart, lungs and kidneys are internal organs.

Oxygen A clear gas that makes up about one fifth of the air we breathe and is essential to all living things.

Particle A tiny piece of matter, or substance.

Pigment A substance that makes, or gives something a particular hue, such as green, or blue.

Puberty The process during which a child turns into an adult.

Saliva A watery substance made in the mouth, also known as spit.

Sensory Linked to the senses (sight, hearing, smell, taste and touch).

Sign language A communication system that uses hand-gestures and signals instead of speech.

Skeletal Relating to the skeleton, or the bones of the skeleton.

Tissue Part of the body, or an organ, made from a group of cells that look the same and do the same thing.

Vaccination To inject someone with a vaccine – a substance that makes the immune system fight against a particular disease.

Vibrations, vibrate Small, fast, shaking movements that are often felt, rather than seen.

Voicebox The organ that makes sounds as you talk or sing, and also controls the volume.

Voluntary An action that you willingly choose or decide to perform.

INDEX